Mahabharata

Compiled by -
S. Chander

ॐ

STEP UP STRINGS

Mahabharata

Compiled by :
S. Chander

First Published : 2003

© S. Chander

ISBN 81-242-0334-2

Published by :
INDIANA
BOOKS
For Crest Publishing House
G-2, 16 Ansari Road,
Darya Ganj, New Delhi - 110 002
326 0651, 326 0618
e-mail : sethidel@del6.vsnl.net.in

Printed at :
Saurabh Print-O-Pack
A-16, Sector-IV, NOIDA (UP)

ॐ

Introduction

The Mahabharata composed between 300 BC and 300 AD has the honour of being the longest epic in the world. The name means the great story of Bharata. Bharata was an early ancestor of both Pandvas and Kauravas.

The story is set in Hastinapur, the capital of the Kurus, identifiable with an area near present Delhi. The ruler of the kingdom namely Dritarastra, had a hundred sons ,who were known as the Kauravas. He had five nephews who were the sons of his brother Pandu, who were called Pandavas. Rivalry emerged between Kauravas and Pandavas due to the refusal of the Kauravas to return the due share of the kingdom back to the Pandavas, which the latter had lost at a game of dice. The

great battle was fought at the field of Kurukshetra, the story of which is told by sage Vyasa.

One of the important aspects of Mahabharata is the teaching of Lord Krishna, which he gave to Arjuna, before the battle of Kurukshetra. This is called the Bhagvad Gita, with means the divine song. Its most important teaching is one should go on doing one's duty, without worrying about the results.

The work is divided in 18 books concerning an 18-day war among eighteen armies. This book provides the reader an insight into the teachings and tenets of this great Indian epic which is not only an epic but has played an integral part in shaping the history of 'Bharata'.

4

Self control is the best way to calm the thought-disturbed mind. It brings serenity and allows us to look on the world dispassionately.

Generally our ignorance clouds this glowing truth.
We reconcile ourselves by blaming fate
for our accidents The learned one knows that
the cause of the accident was some deed
in the past; not fate. He examines his past
behaviour and makes amendments in the future.

... WELL, I SHOULD BLAME SOME PAST DEEDS FOR THE ACCIDENTS ...!!

ACCIDENTS

Do good wherever you can. Do not hesitate
in helpingothers. The person who does good
without looking for a return is at the highest
stage of self-realization. He does not need
any yoga. He does not need any other
form of prayer or renunciation.

෨෨෪෪

The knowledge of Truth brings with it power.
But if the power be mixed with arrogance,
it slides back into ignorance. Power with
humility is the hallmark of the learned one.
He never boasts of his accomplishments or
achievements. Instead he tries
silently to help others.

Though one may be reputed to be a great teacher,
it is his students prowess that will prove the
worth of his teaching. Not just by deeds must he
prove his merit as a great teacher.

The guru stands above all. To him bow the multitude and the king. He is the giver of knowledge. Knowledge is the greatest source of strength.

There is no destruction, for the one who tries to attain perfection either here or hereafter. A transcendentalist is never put to grief. The less evolved unsuccessful one is reborn in the house of the pious and prosperous after attaining heaven and living there for many years.

*Let the laws be read out by a man who
is known to be good and wise.
Though they may be fair and just, to be sure.
If read out by a man, cruel and greedy, they
take on the colours of the man.*

No matter who joins whom in battle, the laws of combat should be fair and just. The king must give his assent to these laws. Both the laws and the king's assent must be published far and wide so that the people know justice rules.

How fortunate are the people with eyes! They curse their misfortune at not having wealth, status and respect. But they do not realize that a blind king who has all these would happily exchange them for vision.

*Begin your work when the hour is calm
and bright, when the stars are holy
and auspicious. Let all men bear witness to the
preparations you make lest they believe
that someone else did it for you.*

Look at the lovely white mansions of the king.
Every one of them bears his coat of arms.
Even a king needs to identify his dwelling
for the easy understanding of his subjects.

The queen and her companions walk about
gorgeously arrayed. Though covered with
exquisite gems, they bow humbly to the poorly
dressed sages, they bow in recognition
to learning, not to wealth.

The people sigh in admiration. Their hearts fill with pride as the king swoops by on a mighty charger, his weapons flashing, the sunrays reflecting off his polished leather gauntlet. It is necessary for a king to appear valorous and mighty.

People utter shout of joy when the king hits
a target. They are silent when another does
the same. This is because they love their king
and love him even more when he
meets their expectations.

Brave and fearless must be the actions of
the king. Quick and light be the movements
of the king. Skilled and true must be the thrust
and parry of his weapons. Then the watching
subjects will be full of admiration
and will adore him ever more.

The greatest warrior must eschew pride.
Full of humility and grace before entering
battle. The conceited warrior forgets
and his arrogance leads him into mistakes.

*The Supreme Truth can be attained by the way
of knowledge. But this path is difficult
and needs tremendous perseverance.
The path of devotion is easier by contrast.*

*Do your duty as a service to the Lord
and see God alone in evertything in a
spiritual frame of mind.*

The king may have many sons but the subjects may not love all of them equally. The king may have many sons but the subjects may not admire them equally. The king may have many sons but the subjects may not respect their learning equally.

*Brothers they may be, but when princes
battle before the cheering subjects, each fights
to win the greater admiration. The restless
crowd shouts encouragement to both.
The battle started in fun turns deadly.*

*The sons of the king may be versed in many arts.
They may be loved, admired and respected by
their subjects. But the son they would prefer to
have rule over them, is the one they respect
for his wisdom and kindness.*

The warrior moves among the people like a tusker in his full glory, like a satiated lion. He towers above them like a cliff. Effortlessly he bears his arms. The people are happy that they have one such to defend them.

20

The King listens to the voice of the people
as they greet his sons. When the voices rise
high like the crescendo of ocean waves,
he must pay greater attention to the
qualities of the prince.

~~~~~~

Watch the prince concentrating on his target.
He sees naught else. The sky, the sun, the tree,
the leaves have all vanished. All that he sees is
the bird he has to pierce. And when he can
concentrate thus, he is successful in his task.

When instead of fighting, the warriors engage
in a battle of words; the mighty smile.
Angry words are a coward's weapon.
The great warrior speaks his anger through
his flaming arrows.

22

*When the king sees flames of wrath and jealous
anger in the eyes of his rival, a
great happiness glows in his proud heart.
He seeks at once the friendship of the one
who could rouse the ire of his rival.
The enemy of the enemy is a potential friend.*

❧❦❧

*What could be a greater come down for a
mighty warrior than to have another perform
the same feats as he? He does not
mind the other's prowess, so much.
Much more, does he mind losing status
in the admiring eyes of his people.*

Challenge is a source of great ire to the proud warrior. He forgets his humility and begins to speak in rude accents thereby lowering himself in the eyes of the wise and saintly.

The king, if not skilled himself, patronises the
one whose deeds are unmatched.
He takes joy in the comradeship of that one.
And still greater joy in the dread
that one's name inspires in his foes.

To enter the martial field, the warrior needs
nothing but strength of his arms and his might.
His right to combat is sanctified by his valour.

Woeful is the mother who sees her sons
fighting on different sides for a cause.
Though she believes in the cause,
she cannot bear to sacrifice one of her sons.
Even though the son may be away from her,
she still loves him true.

The clever king grants wealth and domains
to his mighty friend to arouse his gratitude.
And in return, he seeks only friendship.
It is this friendship which will bring
his mighty friend to fight on
his side during times of adversity.

It is the voice of arrogance that decries the
achievement of a lesser born. By claiming
lineage, an attempt is made to enhance the
value of one's own achievement.
Were a jackal to make a sacrifice
and a tiger to do the same, what difference
would it make to value of the sacrifice?

Great is the hero who does not forget his humble origins. Though his forehead be glistening with the anointments of honour, he does not hesitate to bend it to the dusty feet of his poor father. His father's blessings are more important to him than the jeers of his nobly born enemies.

The warrior who seeks to cow another by insulting him on issues beyond his control (for example, birth) should be discouraged. Bitter taunts ill befit a valorous man. His might should be proved in combat, not in extraneous issues.

It is skill that is to be determined in combat. Strength, perseverance, wit and courage are to be tested in combat. Pride and status are not at issue. So the humblest warrior may engage with the proudest.

When the King announces the swayamvara of
his daughter, may come to vie for her hand.
Many more come to see the fun. And a few come
to incite passions and cause trouble.
They are more dangerous than all the rest.

*When a person is strong, valorous, skilled
and intelligent, why question his lineage?
Like a river's noble course, deeds should
proclaim the warrior. Who wants to know
the river's source?*

*Look at the shining visage of the great warrior,
his eyes bright with intelligence, his strong
shoulders and broad chest. Now do you question
his lineage when he stands before you in
all nobility? Did ever a she-deer breed tordly
tigers in her humble little lair?*

31

The King plants trees, maintains forests, clears path ways and makes fountains of silvery water. These make travel routes sylvan and the travellers are not overcome by weariness.

Even a brother's faith may be swayed.
As long as he believes his brother to be the greatest
warrior, he claims to repose full faith in him.
But when he sees another equally mighty,
his faith turns into half-doubt.

When King assemble to vie for the hand of a
lovely princess, they try to outdo each other in
scattering presents, food,
gold and other wealth. It is the poor who benefit
from it. They bless their lovely princess.

Failure in public can make the greatest hero an object of ridicule. The beggar trembles before the prince. But when the prince is laid low in contest, even the beggar begins to titter.

*When the king wishes to give his daughter
to the most valorous of all without making
enemies of others, he sets the suitors a task.
A task so stupendous that none but the
greatest would even dare to attempt it.*

*Though the contest be among the young and
strong, though the contest be of martial art,
pure and saintly rishis and learned Brahmins
come to the contest to bless it and to resolve
any dispute with their wisdom.*

When a young warrior accomplishes what
other established and renowned warriors
could not, the latter consider it a
personal insult. The saplings of hope in their
hearts shrivel and this they cannot tolerate.

36

See the assembled kings. Lion-chested monarchs,
nobly born princes, chiefs of pure and stainless
name. Give each a seat that befits his status.
A seat wrongly given can sow the
seeds of a great war.

Watch the prince lead forth his sister, the bride,
to the swayamvara. In loud and lofty accents,
he announces to her the names, race,
lineage and deeds of each suitor.
This information helps her
to make her choice.

When a king invites his kinsmen and friends to pay homage at his court, he must receive them with due honour. When honour is smited, a friend becomes an enemy.

When the princess is beautiful, competitors forget their brotherhood. Each looks on the prize as his own and marks his own brother as a foe-man. When the prize is a beautiful princess, the contest becomes a deadly strife.

When a young warrior seeks to achieve what many old and renowned warriors could not, there are some who would discourage rather than cheer him on to attempt the feat. If he listened to them, the warrior would give up even before he started.

The presence of the wise sanctify the holy
sacrifice as the cold valleys are warmed green
by the rays of the spring sun and as
the cool monsoon breeze brings
life to heat baked plains.

40

When a young warrior sets out what other old
and renowned warriors could not,
there are some who encourage him.
They praise his strength. Above
all they praise his lofty will to dare.

When a young warrior sets out to do what
other old and renowned warriors could not,
there are some who encourage him.
They recount to him similar tales of valour.
And thus they stoke the fire of his courage.

The King who aspires to monarchy must look after his subject's needs and wants. He must be unto them like the raindrop nourishing the thirsty ground or like the wide armed tree shading them with its conopy.

When a young warrior accomplishes what
other established and renowned warriors
could not, much ire is aroused in the latter.
Instead of acknowledging the brilliance
of the young, they seek to quash
him by any means available.

When a young warrior accomplishes what other
renowned warriors could not, the latter do not
want to honour his rank or have mercy on
his age. They wish to trample him underfoot
as they would demolish the memory
of an ignominious defeat.

A game of pleasure ought to be played for pleasure alone. If it is used as a serious challenge, it is the easiest way to lose one's very hard earned wealth and kingdom.

44

*When a king amasses his wealth, establishes
the might of his kingdom and makes a name
for himself; he is not content to enjoy it alone.
He invites his kinsmen and friends so that they
may gaze on his creation and pay homage.*

*When a king invites his kinsmen and friends
to show off the might of his court and castle,
surely he sows the seeds of discontent among
them. In time, he will be forced to reap the
harvests of their envy and enmity.*

Do not insult a woman nor ever pull her hair.
With that one act a king's righteous glory is
lost for ever. His ancient and glorious
name is stained for ever.

When a king invites his kinsmen and friends to the holy sacrifice at his court, he must make time to attend to them or appoint sweet tongued, gentle and caring princes to do so.

The desire to demonstrate one's prowess, be it learning, valour or cunning, is strong indeed. As the warriors square off on combat grounds, the musicians compete on the stage and the learned Brahmins in lecture halls.

Beware of the passionate tears in a woman's eye.
They can arouse a mighty surge in the most
timid of men. And in the valorous,
a burning thirst for gory revenge.

48

*Honour is a touchy thing. If all be
honoured equally and simultaneously, those
with greater self opinion feel humiliated.
Yet if one be honoured first,
many of the others feel neglected.*

*When one, brilliant above the rest, is
honoured, the mediocre in the gathering seek
to pull him down by projecting others
equally mediocre. They proclaim their
minor deeds in the great,
loud voice of the majority.*

49

Never seek to stain a woman with deep and dire disgrace. Her ill will and her curses can destroy a hundred brothers and all their sons.

To perform the holy sacrifice and show off his
kingdom, the king needs a very strong ally,
equally if not more powerful. The ally's
influence protects the king from
the wrath of his fellow kings.

The King who aspires to monarchy must ever
guard his kingdom with sleepless eyes.
He must ever tend his subjects with a father's
love and care, knowing their fears
and demolishing their source, rejoicing
with them on occasions of joy.

*Look upon hardships with eagerness. They should not bring tears to the eye.
Look upon them as ordained to serve you, to chesten you through trials and tribulations and finally leave you stronger, healthier, wiser than before.*

When the King aspires to monarchy he must
hold his people within a ring of benevolence.
He must be like the blue sky encompassing all
in its kind dome. He must rule them virtuously,
unimpassionately and humbly.

When a King aspires to monarchy, he should
keep away from games of pleasure like dice.
The challenge of dice can corrupt the sanest
mind, rob the wisest of his throne and the
richest of his wealth.

An insulted person may be quiet during the
day, busy with the numerous chores of life.
It is at night, in the lonesome quiet,
that the emotions torture him and insult
rankles as new in his bosom.

Everyone must be
treated equally irrespective of
relationships. Sages spend life times
searching for this balance.

Take good care of your slave. You do not know
what great passions fiercely scorch his chest.
Were you a slave yourself, vain would be your
wrath and righteous passion, and the inability
would create a raging fire in the mind.

When a woman gives her heart to a man, she does not consider whether his life is long or short, his virtues great or none. Her love is pure and unsullied, untroubled by any material condition.

56

*Though a king may be bountiful, it does not
behave a loyal subject to ask favours forever.
When the needs are satisfied, one should
desist and not keep increasing
the needs and demands.*

*The noble king does not wish to continue
enmity with his kinsmen. He wishes them good
for the evil done and shames them into silence.
Thus does he make them realize his virtue.*

The wise King does not seek war. He seeks first
to converse, to dialogue, to parley. For a war
destroys more than the king. It also decimates
the hapless population, the cattle
and the fields full of grain.

It is said by the wise men of yore that fortune brings no good to mortals who win by wicked wile. And equally, sorrow and deprivation bring no shame to those who are free from sin and guile.

The true and faithful wife fear neither jungle nor exile. Her life may be hard but no dangers will bring woe and sorrows to her. Her sinless deeds and holy conduct spread a charmed circle to hold her safe.

Pride often makes a king underestimate his foe. The foe may not possess the wealth and forces that the king has. But this should not blind the king to his underlying strengths.

60

Greed is a human frailty and kings are subject
to it as much as poor people.
Why else would a king; Famed and noble,
rich with land, tribute and jewels;
Try to steal the cattle of another king?

None should boast of what they cannot achieve.
Called to the challenge, they are forced to seek
wild excuses which convince none and
make them a laughing stock.

At the end of the battle, the field lies purple
with the blood of fallen heroes. Corpses are
piled high, as vultures and jackals feast
on them. The victors try to rejoice but
it is a hollow victory over
empty palaces devoid of life.

But when the foe is cruel and arrogant,
he may consider the wise king's offer of dialogue,
a weakness. In his pride, he may
deem the wise king's mildness as feeble hearted
fear. This in turn will provide good cheer
to his arrogance.

The wise King prays thus to his elders "Be
unto us as a father, loving, not inspired by
wrath. Be unto us a teacher. Show up
the righteous path. If we wander astray,
please set your strong arm
lead us straight".

No battle can be won without commitment of the troops and the leader. Each and everyone must be fully dedicated to the cause. The side which is thus will certainly emerge victorious.

Trust the man who dares speak unpleasant truths on your face. Bear his words in your heart. Remember them. Improve on them. He does a great favour by speaking thus.

The memory of an insult refuses to die down. More so, it thrives on jealousy. Every day, every little act of the speaker (even though it is unrelated) fans the anger of the insulted.

Never allow the enemy's kin to enter your army.
He may pretend devotion to your cause
but his heart will his own on the other side
when you need him most, he may let you down.

The mediator must be transparent and perceived as being above all duplicity in speech and intent. If one warring party feels that he bears a secret love for the enemy and holds a secret grudge against him, the mediations are doomed to failure.

ಬಾಣಜ

An adversary may not possess the arms and armies that a king does. But if hatred lurks in his heart coupled with a bitter desire for revenge it can make him perform unbelievable feats of strength.

A successful King is one who knows the histories of all his subjects. Thus only he can assess their strengths and weaknesses.
Thus only he can determine who is likely to be loyal to him and who may betray him.

Determination must be coupled with patience if
the king wishes to win. Yielding an inch today
may gain a mile tomorrow. Becoming too rigid,
one becomes like the mighty oak that
gets uprooted in a gale.

Old feuds are like potent poisons.
With age, they mature and grow virulent,
From father to son, the hatred is passed
on like life itself, to be cherished and nursed
for the day of revenge.

Evil thoughts do not grow alone in mature heads. They spring up like weeds in the minds of children too. Parents and guardians of such children should keep watch over the development of such children.

Honour is more important to the proud than life itself. A proud king sees his heroes fall one by one. Yet he does not heed the counsel to cease war and sue for friendship.
To him such friendship is stained with pity which pride cannot tolerate.

The king may not heed the advice of his parents while waging war. But it is the parents who suffer most, not only because he perishes on the battlefield. They have to live their last few years on the charity of the victors.

Skill cannot be developed by mere wishing.
The warrior has to practice constantly.
He must think about his goal all the time.
He must concentrate to the exclusion of all else.

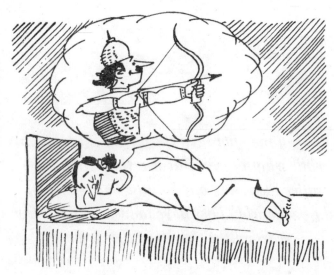

*The heroes who fall in quest of victory or in
defence of their faith are immortalised by bards.
Their tales inspire future generation to pledge
their lives in the same way. Their examples
are cited to stimulate future
generation to acts of glory.*

*The heroes who fall in quest of victory or in
defense of their faith are immortalised by the
bards. But who remembers the widows they
leave behind, some of them taken in the
first flush of youth, some of them
with little children to rear.*

73

The path of knowledge is very difficult but being impartial towards all helps one on this path. It means not having any loved ones or any hated ones. Everyone must be treated equally irrespective of relationships. Sages spend life times searching for this balance.

*In the silent halls of the hardwon palace,
the victorious king treads alone. The only
movements he hears are those of widows whites.
Where are the people with whom he can share
his joy? His exultation gives way to depression.*

*The victorious king cannot give way to
despair on counting the remaining strength of
his people. He must stand up and work towards
rebuilding the kingdom so that people can
flourish and prosper.*

An angry man cannot think coherently.
Incoherent thoughts lead to wrong decisions.
Wrong decisions lead a man astray.

To revive the morale of his subjects, the victorious king must perform religious sacrifices, encourage festivals and celebrate every suitable occasion. Thus he will be able to bring them back to a normal life after the devastations of war.

The leaders must believe in the cause for which they are fighting. Without belief, they will have no inspiration.
Lack of inspiration will be reflected in their behaviour and will demotivate the troops.

Though one may be the son of a noble king but if he is wrathful and strikes terror in the hearts of his subjects, he is not worthy of being the king. The king must be righteous as well as noble.

Mere birth does not make a good king.
If the prince is disrespectful of his elders and
discourteous to young, he is not worthy of
being the king. He must be noble in behavior
as well as in birth.

A King is not determined by the parentage
alone. He must prove his skill and prowess to
win the respect of his people. The king must be
well skilled and well versed in
the art of leadership.

It is not easy to live among material objects and give up all attachment to them. The wise person is not disheartened by failures. He tries again and again till he masters the art. Perseverance and determination are facilitators to the way of success.

Beware of a general who has a hidden agenda.
He will not fight for your cause, your cause is
merely the means for him to achieve his own
objective. He can abandon your cause as easily
as he adopted it.

A man who fights on certain conditions
should not be selected to lead the army.
Who can predict the conditions of battle?
If the situation changes and he refuses to fight,
the army is left headless.

Envy becomes the whole-time companion of the
man who desires material satisfaction.
Whenever he cannot get the things he
wants he is envious of those who have them.
His jealousy binds him to the efforts that
others may have put in or the
costs they may have borne.

*The king must employ different methods to
know the true motivations of his generals.
No one should be trusted blindly to carry
on the cause. Age, years of servitude,
friendliness are no barriers
to going over to the enemy's camp.*

*The mettle of each warrior must be well tested
before he is elevated to the post of commander.
It is not enough for him to be well skilled
in weaponry. He must have strength of will
and fortitude too.*

The most important thing in life is to remain detached from all we do, all the values we practice, all the people with whom we are connected by ties of blood and all the actions which may bring us great honor. One who has been able to do this is the true yogi.

The King should study the mental makeup of the commander of his armies. If he is a man easily swayed by rumours, he must be kept busy so that he has no opportunity to be distracted by rumours.

The past history of commander should be known to the king. He must make every effort to get this information. Hidden in the commander's past may be a secret which can betray the King.

The strong should not be proud. Their strength
has come from God and should be used for good
purposes only. Misused, it will desert them in
the hour of greatest need. Oppressors have
died ignominious deaths because they
did not realize this.

Bravery and cowardice are not the sole possessions of any age or caste. A young man, inexperienced in war, may display great courage or run away in fright. So too, may an old veteran warrior.

Anger is great vice. So too is pride. Together they can destroy a man's common sense. Their explosive combination can even destroy his basic sense of self-preservation.

Do not give anything without considering the need of the taker. Giving should not abuse the dignity of the receiver. It should be in keeping with the welfare of the person and should genuinely uplift him. The real intention of help should be like this.

The flames of envy and jealousy lick at man's anger and keep the heart alive. All the time they remind him of what he should have had but does not have. No man should kindle these flames in another's breast.

Skill is a marvelous thing and it can adorn a humble man as much as it graces a King. The poorest can acquire skills through hard work and constant practice which the prince may not acquire despite much coaching.

The worth of any work lies in the thought which accompanies it and in the method by which it is done. With these, inconsequential work assumes significance because of the remarkable quality of its workmanship.

Woe and misery are relative emotions.
A man may be sorrowing greatly but if he is
told of a greater sorrow of another,
he feels more fortunate and less
miserable by contrast.

It is often said that deprivation for a just cause
is morally fair. Those who say so do not realize
that to deprive, no cause is just
enough or fair enough.

Work is the best way to achieve happiness. But not all work can do so. Only when we work with dedication, care and willingness, we get the pure joy of satisfaction. The effort and sincerity we put in is proportionate to our happiness in its completion.

...OH I'M GETTING THE PURE JOY OF SATISFACTION AFTER COMPLETING THIS WORK!

WORK

All through his life, a King must do good deeds,
dispense justice and help all those who need it.
He does all this to build up a storehouse of good
will for himself which he can call upon
in troubled times.

A King would be shortsighted if he emptied
his treasuries in helping others, He will be
praised while there is money in his coffers.
And laughed at when his
wealth is exhausted.

*For those who worship the Supreme with
unswerving devotion as their personal God,
offer all actions to him, intent on him as
the Supreme, and meditate on him;
he swiftly becomes their savior from the world
that is an ocean of death and transmigration.
True devotion is intense love for God.*

94

It is not enough for a King to build up his armies to crush the enemy. He must learn about the foe's strengths and plan out strategies to exploit his weaknesses.

The ties of marriage are used to seal powerful political alliances. Kings have married their sisters and daughters into powerful clans to assure their support in times of conflict.

Therefore, focus your mind on God, and let your intellect dwell upon him alone through meditation and contemplation. Thereafter you shall certainly attain him. If you are unable to focus your mind steadily on him, then long to attain him by practice of any spiritual discipline; such as a ritual, or deity worship that suits you.

*A man develops best in what interests him.
So one may become a scholar. Another a warrior
of repute. A third into a valiant archer. A
fourth, into a great horseman. Though they
study together, they develop differently.*

*Every effect must have a cause. Most of these
causes can be traced back to a human emotion.
An outraged sensibility can cause a quarrel.
A quarrel can lead to a dispute.
And a dispute to a war.*

Discrimination, Self-knowledge, non-delusion,
forgiveness, truthfulness, control over mind
and senses, tranquility, pleasure, birth, death,
fear, fearlessness, nonviolence, equanimity,
contentment, austerity, charity, fame, disgrace,
all these diverse qualities in human beings
arise from God alone.

Thinking about sensual objects creates in us a great desire to possess them. Any thwarting of these desires kindles the fire of anger in us.

෨෦෮෪

When a man realizes the truth about desire, anger and delusion, he eschews them.
He understands and the need for self-control and begins to practice it diligently.

Self-realization is more difficult for those who fix their minds on an impersonal, unmanifest, and formless Absolute because comprehension of the unmanifest by embodied beings is attained with difficulty.

SELF-REALIZATION IS DIFFICULT FOR ME PERHAPS BECAUSE I DID FIX MY MIND ON UNMANIFEST ABSOLUTE!!

The Truth is this. Our lives are shaped by our deeds. One who realizes this has reached the summit of self-realisation. All his delusions now disappear. He becomes the self-realised one. He serves as an example to those who wish to know the Truth.

When our minds are taken up with thoughts of cars, houses and jewels; we begin to think of them as the final objective of life. This is delusion. A man in the grasp of such delusion cannot think of much else. Nothing appears worthwhile save these.

Self-knowledge is the king of all knowledge,
is the most secret, is very sacred,
it can be perceived by instinct,
conforms to righteousness (Dharma),
is very easy to practice, and is timeless.

The passage of life is not always smooth. Sometimes everything works out well. At others, everything appears to go wrong. He who can face both with indifference is the self-realised one. He does not allow one to fill him with joy and the others with misery.

৪)C৪

Do not hesitate before doing good things. Always remember, that many others will look at your example and at least some of them will follow you. In this way good will spread through the world like ripples in a river.

One who knows God as the unborn, without a beginning or an end, and the Supreme Lord of the universe, is considered wise among mortals, and becomes liberated from the bondage of Karma.

I'M LIBERATED FROM THE BONDAGE OF KARMA BECAUSE I KNOW GOD AS THE SUPREME LORD OF THE UNIVERSE!

There are many who feel that people are different because their values differ from each other. It is not the values but their natures that are responsible for differences in behaviour. Their natures make them look on the world differently.

ČČ

Our natures incline us towards different things. These inclinations nurture desires which in turn make us crave them while leading us away form the Truth.
These inclinations make us dislike the person who tries to show us the truth.
Then we try to avoid him.

The wise surrender to God by realizing-after many births-that everything in the universe and the world is nothing but his manifestation. Such a great soul is very rare.

... EVERYTHING IN THE UNIVERSE AND THE WORLD IS **HIS** MANIFESTATION!

All good and beautiful things in life are born of God. The best of every form of life is his manifestation. His glory shines through all that is wonderful. Remember this when you see anything beautiful, anything that makes you pause in wonder.

There are those who denigrate work by pointing to its mal effects or to circumstances which are unfavorable. The work by itself is neither good nor bad. Our ways of thinking make it so. Any work done well becomes good if its intentions are also good.

The mind is restless and very difficult to control, but it can be subdued by sincere spiritual practice and by detachment.

108

The Self is present equally in all beings. There is no one hateful or dear to God. But, those who worship him with love and devotion are very close to him, and he is also very close to them. Even if the most sinful person resolves to worship him with single-minded loving devotion, such a person must be regarded as a saint because of making the right resolution. His devotee shall never perish or fall down.

Whosoever desires to worship whatever deity-using whatever name, form, and method-with faith, God makes their faith steady in that deity. Endowed with steady faith they worship that deity, and obtain their wishes through that deity. Those wishes are granted by him.

The highly evolved unsuccessful one does not go to heaven, but is born in a spiritually advanced family. A birth like that is very difficult to obtain in this world. There, one regains the knowledge acquired in previous life, and strives again to achieve perfection. The most devoted of all is the one who lovingly remembers God with faith.

Thought of whatever object that predominates during one's lifetime, one remembers that object at the end of life and achieves it. Do not set your mind on the Supreme Being but set Him as your ultimate Goal.

This divine power (Maya), consisting of three states of mind or matter, is very difficult to overcome. Only those who surrender unto God easily, cross over this Maya.

ॐ

Titles in
STEP UP SERIES

ॐ